MW01174801

Investing For Beginners

An Intelligent Investor's Guide to Growing Your Wealth and Retiring Early

Copyright 2018 by Walter Wayne - All rights reserved.

This document is geared towards providing exact and reliable information in regards to the topic and issue covered. The publication is sold with the idea that the publisher is not required to render accounting, officially permitted, or otherwise, qualified services. If advice is necessary, legal or professional, a practiced individual in the profession should be ordered.

- From a Declaration of Principles which was accepted and approved equally by a Committee of the American Bar Association and a Committee of Publishers and Associations.

In no way is it legal to reproduce, duplicate, or transmit any part of this document in either electronic means or in printed format. Recording of this publication is strictly prohibited and any storage of this document is not allowed unless with written permission from the publisher. All rights reserved.

The information provided herein is stated to be truthful and consistent, in that any liability, in terms of inattention or otherwise, by any usage or abuse of any policies, processes, or directions contained within is the solitary and utter responsibility of the recipient reader. Under no circumstances will any legal responsibility or blame be held against the publisher for any reparation, damages, or monetary loss due to the information herein, either directly or indirectly.

Respective authors own all copyrights not held by the publisher.

The information herein is offered for informational purposes solely, and is universal as so. The presentation of the information is without contract or any type of guarantee assurance.

The trademarks that are used are without any consent, and the publication of the trademark is without permission or backing by the trademark owner. All trademarks and brands within this book are for clarifying purposes only and are owned by the owners themselves, not affiliated with this document.

Table of Contents

Introduction

Dear Reader,

First and foremost, I would like to thank you for purchasing this book. Whether this is your first step into learning more about investing and growing your wealth or a continuation of your journey, I hope it provides you value.

This book contains information on the fundamentals of investing and its importance as well as how to get started on growing your wealth and avoiding common pitfalls that beginners run into. It is targeted for beginners to get familiar with investing rather than dealing with intricate investment strategies. Also, I would like to add that you will not find anything in this book to get you rich overnight because that simply does not exist. It is important to remember that investing is not the same as gambling. People who have that misconception are the ones who fail the fastest.

While many investing and finance books can be bogged down with complicated financial terms and other fluff that makes it difficult to get past the first few chapters, this book is deliberately to the point and easy to follow.

I hope you enjoy and benefit from it. Feel free to leave a review if you do!

Regards,

Walter Wayne

Chapter 1: Why Invest?

What the rich do differently

Stretching your paycheck to make ends meet at the end of the month can sometimes be quite tricky. Most people feel that they are never earning enough or living life to the fullest. No one would mind having more money. Whether you are someone living paycheck to paycheck or are already a millionaire, having more money (legally of course!) is hardly ever a bad thing.

But why are some people so much better off than others? What do the rich do differently? You may be asking yourself these questions from time to time. Before answering these questions, it is important to note that when I say someone is rich, I don't mean that they make an absurd amount of income. Rather, their net worth (assets minus liabilities) is very high. Having a high net worth shows that you understand the game of money and how to retain what you make rather than spend it all. This is the reason why I don't consider lottery winners as being rich. Until they can prove that they can either retain the money they won or grow it rather than be broke a few years later, they are not rich in my eyes.

It might seem as if some people are just destined to be wealthy but that is simply not true. The difference between the rich and the rest of society is the difference in mindset regarding money. They understand how to make money work for them rather than working for it. A truth universally acknowledged is that the rich save and invest a portion of their income first. Only after they have set aside enough money for their goals do they spend. They are willing to sacrifice short term pleasure for long term gain. As we will get into later, this is an important idea to embrace when investing.

On the other hand, the lower and middle classes do the exact opposite. They often avoid investing because it means they cannot spend their paychecks right away and enjoy the pleasure from it. They conform to materialism and all their savings are used for various (and usually unnecessary) purchases that bring about instant gratification.

For example, let's say two people, one having a middle class mindset and the other one having a wealthy mindset, both win $70,000 from a contest. The middle class mindset is immediately going to start shopping the market for a brand new luxury car while the wealthy mindset is immediately going to start looking for an investment opportunity.

The middle class mindset finds a beautiful luxurious car while the other finds a beautiful and safe investment. This beautiful car depreciates 15% annually for 8 years while the beautiful investment generates 10% annually for 8 years. At the end of the 8 years, the car is worth $17,349 while the investment is worth $128,616. This is a very practical example as to why and how the rich get richer.

Being poor has nothing to do with someone else being rich. We all can be financially independent and retire early if we develop the right mindset and abilities then put them into action.

Making your money work for you

The main idea behind investing is to use your money to make more money. Although this sounds simple as an idea, it is not so easy to implement. This will be explained in further detail when talking about common beginner mistakes as well as the role that emotions play in investing.

Saving, let alone investing, is hard enough for most people. You can save parts of your paycheck for some short-term goals, like a holiday or a car much more easily because there is a tangible reward as your goal. To make investing easier you have to develop the appreciation that your money is generating more wealth and leading you to financial independence.

A concept that keeps me excited about investing is the idea that I can be making money all the time regardless of whether I am working or not. Coming from an employee background originally, I have always traded my time for my money. Work 40 hours a week and get paid. If you don't put in those hours, no one is paying you. With investing, however, you don't have to trade any hours for money. Even if you're lounging on the beach enjoying a nice sunny day, you can be making money.

You sit every day at work and earn money for your employer. At the beginning or the end of each month, you get a paycheck and it allows you to provide for you and your family as well as fulfill some short term goals you may have. However, you also have some long-term goals which you would love to fulfill before retirement.

You have two choices: you can either maintain your spending habits or you can invest that amount and watch it make you even more money. Now I'm not saying that you need to deprive yourself of life's pleasures. Even if money is scarce or you are a big spender, you can start investing with a small amount. You do not need to have thousands of dollars to get started. Even just one part of your paycheck can help you earn enormous amounts of money given enough time.

Therefore, investing proves to be a fantastic choice for any individual. Making your money work for you can result in doubling your savings many times over. In this age, investing is the only reliable way of growing your wealth.

Your paycheck has a lot of potential, and it can take you a lot further than you might think. By setting aside a small percentage of your paycheck each month and investing it, you can reach your future goals without putting a strain on your current lifestyle, and the best part about it is that the money you invest will constantly make you more money. Whether you are sleeping, eating, partying, or spending time with your loved ones – you will get richer every year.

A question you may have is that what about market crashes. How can you get richer if the market is going down? Although I won't go into detail about it in this book, market crashes actually can be a blessing. They present great buying opportunities for the intelligent investor because they are eventually always followed by a recovery that takes the market to new heights. These are known as bear and bull markets, respectively.

You don't need to have a multimillion dollar business or properties all over the world to be wealthy. It is possible to invest parts of your savings and paychecks and witness incredible results over time.

Also, investing does not require you to have any sort of specific knowledge that can only be learned in some top business school. By simply applying the fundamentals, anyone can have huge success.

The danger of inflation

Many people believe that keeping their savings in the bank will keep their capital secure. However, in this time and age, savings rates are low, and they yield fewer gains than they used to. They also forget about the eroding power of inflation or simply don't even know what it is.

A savings account is best used for short-term goals and emergency funds. In case you don't know, an emergency fund is money that you put aside in case of a rainy day. It should contain about 6 months' worth of your paycheck in case of an emergency such as getting laid off or any other circumstance because of which you cannot work for some time.

In case you don't know what inflation is, it is the decrease in the purchasing value of money. For example, 40 years ago you could buy a Big Mac from McDonald's for $0.75 and now it is no less than $5.00 for the same burger. Did their costs go up? Probably. But that wouldn't justify a price increase of over 6x. The reason for this price increase is due to inflation. Since money is constantly being printed by the government, there is a larger supply of it every year therefore the value of it decreases.

It is vital to remember that inflation is always at work. It erodes your savings, and it makes your money lose value gradually. By keeping it in your bank account with an interest rate below 3%, which is the average inflation rate at the time of writing, you will be losing money.

Instead, by investing your money rather than just saving it, it will be secured under an "investment blanket" that will beat inflation. Once you understand that by only saving, you are actually losing money every year, the need to invest becomes much more evident. The wealthy understand this very well.

They will keep their money in a bank only if they haven't found a valuable investment. Until then they practice patience, and once an opportunity arises, they swiftly take the money out and invest it.[12]

---

[1] http://dollarsandsense.my/why-most-rich-people-dont-have-much-cash-in-their-bank-accounts/

[2] https://www.thebalance.com/how-does-inflation-affect-bank-accounts-315771

Investing in yourself

By far, the most important investment you could make is in yourself and I congratulate you for taking that step by reading this book.

Opening a business is not a valuable investment if you do not know how to run it. Likewise, investing in stocks, bonds, real estate, and other financial instruments doesn't mean that you will experience success - unless you know what you are doing.

Therefore, before trying to amass your wealth, think about your life. See what your good and bad qualities are, what you can accomplish, how much stress you can handle, and so on. Most people think that wanting something should be enough - that the universe will just give it to them because they deserve it.

And most people do deserve to have enough money so that they never have to think about it. Yet, it is not as easy as it seems. Successful investors didn't just wake up one day as millionaires or buy a few shares of a stock and become rich in a couple of weeks. They put the work in, they studied, and they developed their skills. They tried to be the best in their respective fields, knowing that the risks and effort would pay off. This doesn't apply to just investing but to life in general. To get where you want to go, you must put in the work.

As you improve yourself, your skills, and your willingness to learn, you will also develop the ability to grow your wealth.

Key points

- Invest first, spend after. Develop a "wealthy mindset".
- Make money work for you instead of only you working for money.
- Inflation erodes your savings.
- The most important investment is in yourself.

Chapter 2: The Power of Compounding

Growing your wealth: slowly but surely vs. overnight

We would all like to become millionaires overnight. We want it to be just like winning a lottery: you buy a ticket, and suddenly, you are rich. You think of the next Uber and suddenly you are making millions.

But, the chances of that happening are quite slim. What's more, growing your wealth overnight shouldn't be your goal. In fact, if we go back to the lottery example, most lottery winners tend to end up broke within a few years of winning and in a pile of debt because they do not understand the game of money.

Rome wasn't built in a day. In the same way, you cannot expect an incredible surge of money in the beginning. As we will learn with compounding, the returns from your investments are typically underwhelming in the beginning compared to the principal you put in. However, we will also learn that the returns can become overwhelming given enough time.

Especially when it comes to investing, it is crucial to take your time and think about your options. The most successful investors are the ones who have used investment strategies for an extended period of time. They didn't try to do it overnight. Instead, they first invested in themselves, their knowledge, and their skills. Afterward, they took their money and placed it into smart investments.

Even though investing can have a fair amount of uncertainty, there are ways to deal with it. Your mind and knowledge should be your greatest strengths. And, in time, your investing experience will help you make better decisions. A very important tip to keep in mind is to only invest with what you can afford. Do not use loans to invest, your kids' college funds, or any sort of capital that you can't afford to lose. As we will learn in later chapters, keeping your emotions in check is just as important as the knowledge aspect of investing. And if you are emotionally attached to the money you are investing, you are much more likely to fail.

It is very important to start saving and investing early on but it is equally important to not rush into any investments. Once you learn more about the market you are interested in, and you feel like you have analyzed the best potential investments, only then should you consider making an investment.

During that process, you should practice patience. It is always better to start slowly and avoid huge losses than to risk it all on something, get burnt, and develop a fear of investing.

Compounding: how to successfully grow your wealth

Compounding is a phenomenon that can grow your wealth exponentially. It doesn't require you to think about it too much. Your job is to make an initial investment - you place your principal amount of money into something you believe in and let time do the work for you.

Albert Einstein once mentioned that compound interest is the eighth wonder of the world. The person who understands it will be able to earn it. Otherwise, he would have to pay it. This goes back to the fact about the wealthy making money work for them while the rest work for money. In other words, compounding can either work for you by generating wealth from your investments or it can deplete your wealth via debt.

If you are given a choice between taking a million dollars or taking a penny and having it double every day, which would you take? Another twist we can add is that if you take the penny doubling route then you can change your mind before the 9th day. Over 90% of people choose the million dollars because they do not understand the power of compounding. Choosing the penny doubling route leads to $5,368,709.12 versus the $1,000,000!

Now let's say you try the penny route for 8 days. On the 8th day you would finally make your first dollar, an overwhelming $1.28! Many people here would panic thinking they made the wrong choice and opt for the million instead. However, by the 16th day, that $1.28 is now $327.68; by the 24th day, it is $83,886.08; and by the 30th day, it is $5,368,709.12. It is important to understand that the process starts off slow but once it picks up, the results are amazing. This is the power of compounding at play.

Although the example is extreme since your rate of return is 100% (doubling) and it is compounded daily (doubling every day), this phenomenon can still do wonders for your finances. In other words, compounding helps explain why investing is so powerful and necessary.

On the other hand, compound interest is your worst enemy if you have a significant amount of debt. This is why many individuals still have trouble paying off their credit card bills, which can easily ruin their credit score. The same principles of compound interest apply but it is now working against you.

When you get your credit card bill, it is vital to pay it off in total as soon as possible. Otherwise, the interest could add up and, in the end, you will have to pay a much larger sum than what was originally there.

Still, when it comes to large purchases such as mortgages and cars, usually you cannot pay them off immediately. To avoid compounding working against you, pay as much as you can above the bare minimum installment every month. Paying off debt can be thought of as a form of investing that has a guaranteed interest rate which is often very hard to promise with other investments. Instead of generating positive dollars (standard investments), you eliminate generation of negative dollars (debt). The net effect on your wealth is the exact same.

For a beginner that is new to investing, this is one of my first recommendations. Sure, you can make some safe small investments in the beginning but allocate most of the capital to pay off your debts. It's important to note that this is dependent on the interest rate of your debts as well. For example, if you have credit card debt with 20% interest then it is vital to pay that off right away. The same applies with other high interest rate debt. This because you are unlikely to find an investment that will *guarantee* a return of the same magnitude.

It is important to ask oneself whether a guaranteed investment with the same interest rate can be found. As a beginner, it can be difficult to gauge this but as a general rule of thumb, I would recommend paying off any debts with over 6% interest rate as soon as possible.

By understanding compounding and learning how to invest, you can easily retire with much more than you thought possible. However, for compounding to work, you have to keep that money invested. You can't make a decent return one year then decide to buy a new TV with the interest you earned because you would have to restart the entire compounding process.

Let's look at an example using the stock market where we keep our returns invested. You have $10,000 you can invest and decide to invest it in the stock market. You are able to earn a 10% rate of return every year

At the end of year 1, you have $11,000. You reinvest the $1,000 profit. The next year, you have $12,100.

Now, imagine you start investing and reinvesting like this in your 20s. Your main goal is to retire at 65, and if you start at the age of 25, you have 40 years to earn your wealth.

If you collect the earnings and don't reinvest them, after forty years, you will have made only $50,000 in total. However, if you continuously reinvest after forty years, your ending balance will be $452,592.56! Note that only the initial $10,000 is invested and no more is added to the initial principal amount from your own pocket. Once you see these numbers, it begins to make sense how the wealthy get so much more ahead of the middle and lower classes.

Now what if you had started at age 20 or 30 instead? If you had invested at age 20, you would have $728,904.84! From age 30, you would have $281,024.37! This is why it is so important to start as early as possible.

How to successfully use compounding to your advantage

When it comes to compounding, most people don't have the patience to stay invested and wait. They are in the mindset of making lots of money as quickly as possible. However as illustrated previously, it is important to develop the discipline to keep as much of your money invested as you can and not access those funds unless there is an emergency (and your emergency fund runs out) or you feel you have enough to retire comfortably. This allows you to use compounding to its full potential.

However, to illustrate the benefits further, I am going to use a real-life example.

A woman named Grace Groner started investing in her twenties. After college, she got a job as a secretary, and she remained there for more than four decades.

Her salary was an average salary. Therefore, in order to earn more money and grow her wealth, she bought three shares of the company where she worked. They were about $60 per share, which makes her investment about $180.

Grace Groner never sold her shares. Instead, she kept them for 75 years and collected the dividends (A dividend is a sum of money that is paid to shareholders from the company's profits. Each share has an associated dividend attached to it. However, not all companies pay a dividend). Furthermore, she then continuously reinvested those dividends, and when she passed, her total investment was worth $7 million.

It is important to remember that the company in question experienced a rather steady growth throughout the years. They grew about 14.97% each year, which makes the original share prices a real bargain. Yet, Grace probably didn't know that - she just believed in long-term investing.[3]

---

[3] http://www.investinganswers.com/education/time-value-money/how-one-normal-lady-turned-200-7-million-3874

Key points:

- Be realistic with your results. You cannot get rich overnight.
- Compounding takes time but the results make it very much worthwhile.
- Compounding either works for you or against you. You have the power to control this.

Chapter 3: Important Principles of Investing

Investing vs. speculating

You might have heard some people use these terms as synonyms. However, there is an important difference between investors and speculators.

For starters, investors like Warren Buffett have built their entire business empires through investing alone. They use fundamental analysis to determine whether they should allocate their money into a particular investment.

That means they had to examine the investment's potential, as well as risks they might run into. For example, when evaluating a company, its financial strength and management are vital factors, but you must also look at the competition, the state of the respective industry, and possible macroeconomic factors. Do not worry about all this right now. This is just being mentioned to show that investing is not so easy as clicking a few buttons.

We could call this investing rather than speculating because it doesn't involve fast, speculative short-term moves. Unlike speculators, investors thrive when they find an investment that will pay off in the future. Thus, they have the ability to hold their investments for a long time, sometimes even for decades. Through fundamental analysis, they know it will pay off rather than hoping it will.

When it comes to speculators, things are a bit different. We usually see speculators in every type of market. They opt for short term market moves, hoping that their investments will increase in value rather than doing fundamental analysis and knowing that their investments will increase in value. The aim is usually to gain quick profit by buying and selling in a short amount of time.

It is needless to say that this is a far riskier strategy. Speculation may work occasionally, but in the long term, it is not viable. Remember that investing is not gambling. It is meant to be slow and steady.

According to Benjamin Graham, from whom Warren Buffett first learned about investing, "an investment operation is one which, upon thorough analysis, promises safety of principal and a satisfactory return. Operations not meeting these requirements are speculative."

Principal protection

The principal is the original amount of money you have placed in an investment. Anything above that counts as earnings.

Warren Buffett didn't stay rich just because life wanted it that way. He maintained his wealth with a set of two rules: "Rule No. 1: Never lose money. Rule No. 2: Never forget rule No.1".

That might sound simple and obvious, yet it is not so easy to implement in practice. When it comes to investing, especially in the beginning, it is important not to get greedy for returns and in turn, put your principal at risk. It is much easier to lose money than to make money if you are not careful.

I like to compare this idea to exercising and nutrition. Let's say you go to the gym and exercise with full intensity for 2 hours. You run on the treadmill for a gruelling 40 minutes and do weightlifting for another 80 minutes. At the end of it, you're exhausted. Now you go home and are ready to have a well-deserved meal. However, if you decide to have a couple of cheeseburgers, which you can eat within 10-15 minutes, then much of that hard work you did in the gym for 2 hours goes right down the drain.

Comparing this to investing, let's say you buy some real estate at the beginning of the year, its price goes up by 20% by the end of the year, and you decide to sell. Now you take that money and decide to invest it in a stock. This stock is risky due to the uncertain outlook of the industry but it offers the chance at significant returns. A couple weeks later, some bad news comes out about the industry as a whole and your stock goes down by 40%. Now the earnings that took an entire year to make are gone along with some of your principal. All within a couple of weeks.

Invest in what you know

If you have worked with technology your whole life then invest in tech-related businesses. If you are in construction and have lots of exposure to houses or commercial properties then go into real estate related investments. If you feel you do not have enough knowledge in any particular area, then make sure to learn about it in detail before investing.

Warren Buffett defines risk as "not knowing what you're doing." Therefore, the most obvious way to limit risk is to know as much as you can about your investment.

Do your homework

There is no magical investment that will automatically make you tons of money without having to put any work into it. There are some investments that require minimal work, as we will learn later, but even then, some minimum research must be done.

For every investment you make, you must have at least a few fundamental reasons that will help you stick with it even if there is short term volatility. The more reasons you can gather for your investment, the easier it is to stick with it for the long term.

Be patient and choose your investments carefully

I have already shown you how powerful compounding is. However, in order for it to work, you have to learn to be patient.

The power of patience is a vital tool when it comes to investing. Your investments will not pay off if you constantly fret about them. Selling and buying whenever the market drops or performs well, respectively, will not help you amass your wealth.

Short term performance should not have any impact on your investment decisions. Most people panic if something does not go the way they expected it right away. So long as the fundamental reason for your investment has not changed, there is no need to panic.

If you have done the proper analysis and know your investment, then all you have to do is be patient and wait for the results. As they say, slow and steady wins the race.

Many people associate activity with success. If you are not constantly investing, then you are falling behind. Investing actually does not involve much activity at all. You should not be investing in whatever opportunity comes in front of you. It is important to be critical about every opportunity. If you stick to a set of criteria and certain standards, only a few investments should be worth investing in.

Opportunity cost is an important concept to understand that helps to limit the number of investments you make. Every investment decision you make has an associated opportunity cost tied to it. In the simplest terms, it is the cost of a missed opportunity. If you invest in something, it means you are giving up an investment in something else. Therefore, you must be sure that whatever you are investing in is better than all the other potential choices. So, not only do you have to make sure that your investment is excellent on its own, but also that it is better than the other potential options.

On the flip side, however, it is important not to be too strict and pass up on every opportunity that comes your way just because you feel that there may be a better opportunity out there. Most of them though, you should pass on. But when you finally do find an opportunity that meets your strict standards and is better than the other options available, you should invest heavily into it.

Quality vs. cheapness

When it comes to investing, we want to make sure we are getting quality at a fair price. Overpaying for high quality will result in low returns and underpaying for poor quality could lead to loss of principal. Thus, a balance has to be reached. This comes with thorough analysis as well as experience.

A common tip for beginners that I hear often is to begin by investing in a company/stock that you love. Most likely, you love the company because it makes great products which would indicate that it is a quality company but that does not mean it is fairly priced. Although this is better than investing in speculative stocks, there are usually much better options.

Key points:

- Think like an investor, not a gambler.
- Rule No.1 is to never lose money. Rule No.2 is to never forget Rule No.1.
- Invest in what you know and have solid reasons for why you are investing in a certain investment by conducting the proper research.
- Once you are sure on an investment, be patient and think for the long term.
- High activity does not equal high results.
- Aim for high quality at a fair price.

Enjoying the book? Leave a review and let me know your thoughts!

Chapter 4: Know Yourself and Your Investment

What kind of personality do you have?

As a beginner, this chapter can be tempting to not take as seriously as the rest. You may be thinking that you know yourself and can keep your emotions under control. However, it's important to note that even the best investors can have trouble with this. It is one of those things that seems very easy and simple to understand in theory but is actually difficult to apply in practice.

When first starting out, many of the technical aspects of investing may not make sense right away but the psychology and emotion behind investing is something that most people can grasp fairly easily. Therefore, pay careful attention to this chapter because if you can understand and apply this, then over half the battle is won.

You have to take your personality into consideration. Are you a typically anxious person? Do you hate making decisions? Are you prone to emotional reactions?

If your answer is yes to any of these questions, investing might not be the best option for you naturally. However, you can always change yourself for the better. Anxiety is something that could easily ruin your investing strategy, but it can also make you more cautious than others. You are generally better than most at being aware about the details and making sure everything about the investment is excellent. However, it can be hard to make the decision to proceed.

On the other hand, if you are more prone to being emotional, then you may have the problem of over action. As mentioned before, it is important to understand that more activity does not mean more success in investing. It is important to set up a strict of criteria that you base your investments on and only make decisions if that set of criteria is met. This helps to keep things more technical and less emotional.

Making decisions is one of the most important steps in investing. You have to carefully consider all factors and reach a conclusion about whether a certain investment is worth buying into or if an existing investment should be sold. It can be stressful and you should know if you can handle it.

Can you be as emotionless as possible?

Gaining a profit or losing money is going to trigger a variety of emotions in you. You could easily become ecstatic or angry, and both positive and negative emotions can take a toll on you.

Because of this, most investors try to be as emotionless as possible. This is especially true when it comes to long term investors.

Holding investments that you feel strongly about for an extended period of time helps to reduce your stress levels. You have done your research and determined that it is a valuable investment. Therefore, you know that any short term price fluctuations are just noise.

Being emotionless is a valuable trait in the investing market. By setting your feelings aside, you will nurture clear thinking and make better decisions.

Hot-headed investors have a higher chance of losing all of their money. In contrast, those who are patient and calm can easily determine whether any price fluctuations are worth attention.

Controlling your emotions

It is easier said than done, but controlling your emotions is a crucial part of investing. Markets go up and down every day. You must be able to stay calm and composed.

Even if the prices of his or her investments go down, an emotionless and intelligent investor will stay calm and ignore it as long as the value of the investment and his fundamental reasons stay intact.

However, if controlling emotions is not something you are good at (and you recognize and admit that, which can be difficult), then passive investing like an index fund is your best option. This will be explained in more detail later.

Know your investment

Although this was mentioned previously, it is important to mention it again in this chapter because it has such a large impact on helping to deal with emotions.

Warren Buffett has said to only invest in your circle of competence, which is what you know and are familiar with. More importantly, you must recognize what you don't know and either try to avoid it or learn more if you want to invest in it.

Smart investors are the ones who recognize when something has potential and when it doesn't. They use rational thinking instead of trends. Following the herd is not a very good way of earning money and amassing wealth. Remember that to be above average, you must stray away from what is average. Although it can be emotionally straining, the payoff is worth it.

By investing in what you know and having strong fundamental reasons behind every investment, it is much easier to keep your emotions in check and make logically sound decisions.

Key points

- Be brutally honest with yourself. Are you an emotional person?
- Can you control your emotions?
- Knowing your investments helps to keep emotions in check.
- If you feel you cannot control your emotions well enough, then a passive investing strategy is recommended.

Chapter 5: Common Beginner Mistakes

Inevitably, you will make mistakes in your investing journey but it is important to learn from each error, understand why it happened, and what you could have done differently. Even the most successful investors have made mistakes in their careers. In fact, some of their mistakes were large enough to cost them their entire fortunes but they had the resilience and mental toughness to bounce back. However, an even better method than learning from your own mistakes is to learn from others' mistakes. Therefore, I have provided some common mistakes that beginners tend to make.

Gambler's Mentality

As I have preached many times during this book, investing is not the same as gambling and speculating. The idea is not to get rich overnight. Rather, get rich slowly and steadily. Avoid any investments that seem too exciting or offer returns that seem too good to be true. Chances are that they are not. If investing turns out not to be as exciting as you thought, chances are you're doing it right.

Buying high, selling low

Beginners do not have enough experience at first to rationally handle a sharp price decline. Hence, they often start panic selling because fear takes over.

We all like to preach the idea of buying low and selling high but more often than not, the opposite is true. Due to the role that emotions play, it is challenging to buy when prices are going down and easy to buy when they are going up. A large part of this is due to certain biases and pattern recognition systems that we have in our brain. For example, if the price of a stock is going up, our brain feels as if it will keep going up. The same applies for when the price is going down.

This brings us back to being emotionless. If you practice tuning out your emotions, and practice reasoning through proper analysis and research instead, you will never get into a state of panic. On the contrary, you will be happy when the price goes down because it just means you can buy even more at an even lower price.

Not understanding your investment

Your best friend gives you a tip about a local business that is for sale. The owner is retiring and he wants to sell it fast so he offers to sell at a low price. You've never shopped there before and don't know much about it. You do know though that it is always busy and that business seems to be good. Should you buy it? If you do enough research to learn about the business and how it works then maybe. But then you also have to confirm the financials of the business and see if it really is making solid profits. Only once you are confident it works rather than hoping it will work, should you invest. This same logic can and should be applied to any investment you make.

Not enough research

I'll repeat this briefly one more time. Never go blindly into any investment and hope that something will go right. You should have confidence that it will go right. This doesn't mean that you have to be 100% confident that it will, but the probability should be highly in your favour.

Not planning ahead

Making an investment plan might not sound exciting but it could significantly help you on your way to achieving early retirement.

Just like with marketing plans, investment plans need to be detailed and tailored to your own needs. You cannot simply say: "I want to make a lot of money."

Therefore, before investing in a variety of financial instruments, it is vital to list your primary goals. How much would you like to earn? Have you thought through your upcoming investments? How much risk are you willing to take and how much can you actually handle? What is your time horizon? List what you aim to accomplish, and you will easily focus on that.

Under diversification

One of the most important components of your investing career should be diversification. To put it simply - do not put all of your eggs in one basket.

For example, in terms of stocks, you might be interested in technology specifically. However, if you invest and reinvest in the same sector all the time, that would mean that all your assets are in one area. Thus, if something happens in the technology sector that causes prices to plummet, you would suffer major losses.

Hence, creating a diversified portfolio should be one of your goals. There should be some diversification at all levels of your asset classes (stocks, bonds, real estate, etc. are all different asset classes). For example, in your stock portfolio you should have a few stocks in the same sector as well as stocks in other sectors. Furthermore, you could invest in smaller companies as well as some large companies.

Another example could be in real estate. You could buy different types of properties such as single story homes, duplexes, apartments, etc. You could go into commercial real estate or even purchase properties in different cities.

Lastly, you should try to invest in many different asset classes which we will talk about in the next chapter. Developing a thorough investment plan will help with identifying what is best for you.

Over diversification

It is easy to get caught up in diversification. It is one of the concepts that I hear the most about in investing. There are a few problems with diversification however. One is that it becomes difficult to keep track of all your investments when you have too many of them. Secondly, it leads to average returns. It is highly unlikely that you have as the utmost confidence in all the investments you make therefore many of them will end up performing poorly because you just invested in them for the sake of diversification. This ends up watering down the results from the investments that have performed well (since you researched them thoroughly). Therefore, like everything, it is important to find a balance in diversification. Invest in enough different assets so that the risk is spread out but not at the expense of your returns. For example, in stocks, owning 15 to 20 stocks at a time is more than enough.

Being impatient

Your emotions can lead to a surge of impatience if you see many people investing in something; you don't want to miss out on it. You may even sell one of your best investments that is just performing poorly in the short term but will eventually gain momentum. Next thing you know, the hyped-up investment is down 30% while the one you sold is now up 20%.

Patience is a virtue you should nurture. Long-term investments pay off after some time and result in much less stress. Jumping from one investment to another is a clear sign of an impatient investor.

Overconfidence

I'm not saying you shouldn't have faith in your own investing abilities. Confidence is vital if you want to be successful. Yet, there is something to be said about overconfidence. It can substantially hinder us and blur our minds. You might think that a certain investment has potential. Since you've been on a winning streak, you feel confident you are right about this as well. So, you decide to not do the proper research and just invest anyway. This will likely not end in a good result. You might get lucky and that certain investment works out but if you make it a habit, eventually it will catch up to you.

Investing with money you can't afford to lose

The easiest way to bring fear, greed and other negative emotions onto yourself is by investing with money you cannot afford to lose. You are emotionally connected to that money which leads to poor decisions as discussed previously. Investing with money that you don't absolutely need will result in you being much more relaxed and in turn, will lead to much better investing decisions.

Chapter 6: Where to Start?

What can you invest in?

You have probably heard of asset classes before this book. Most financial securities are bundled up together, and the classes are based on their similarity.

Here are the five general ones most people invest in:

Stocks or equities. When you buy a stock, you are buying a part of that company and thus becoming a shareholder.

Real Estate. You can buy either residential or commercial property. Most funds focus on commercial, but you can always buy residential properties or commercial properties yourself as well. With the second option, you have many different choices such as flipping, repairing and selling, renting out, etc. The barrier for entry is higher however since more capital is needed.

Cash. This also includes cash equivalents. These are generally quite low yielding (your savings account for example) and should generally only be used for the short term.

Commodities. This includes a variety of investments, such as oil and gas. Furthermore, you can also invest in precious and industrial metals, as well as agricultural commodities. Just like stocks, these are heavily influenced by supply and demand.

Bonds. Also known as fixed income securities. Most of them are issued by the government or by companies who need investors to fund them. Simply put, you are giving out a loan which is paid back over a term you choose and with an interest rate dependant on the time frame, risk associated with the bond, and interest rates set by a governing body such as the Federal Reserve. They generally offer lower returns but are also much less risky compared to other investments.

What is the best choice for beginners?

By now, you already know that investing doesn't have to be complicated. Yet, it is crucial to keep learning and familiarizing yourself with as much investing material as possible. For many of you, this may be the first investing book you pick up but it should not be the last. Hopefully you have gained some knowledge on the fundamentals of investing but there is still lots to learn if you want to maximize your potential.

In my opinion, investing in stocks is the best option for you as long as you have a long enough time horizon (at least 10 years). They offer the best returns in return for the low amount of relative work they require relative to other investments. Furthermore, they do not require you to have a large amount of capital to get started. You can easily get started with as little as $1000.

You can begin by following your favorite companies as well as different companies that have a history of consistent earnings and a strong economic moat. Immerse yourself in the investing culture. Once you gain more knowledge and are able to decide which company is the best one for you, you can start putting your money into it.

Although this book won't go into details on how to pick stocks and how to evaluate companies, you have the basic fundamental knowledge on what you will need to look for and what to be wary of. In the meantime, while you are learning, begin by investing in index funds which require minimal research since they contain a basket of companies and follow the market.

An index fund is basically a collection of stocks that follow a certain market index. For example, the S&P 500, which consists of the top 500 biggest companies in America based on market cap, is a market index. When people are talking about beating the market, they are talking about a certain index.

When it comes to stocks, everyone wants to beat the market but what many don't realize is that only 50% of people can beat the market because there have to be 50% that don't. Therefore, if you simply track the returns of the market and match them, then you are automatically beating 50% of people. Considering that many of those people are professionals on Wall Street with fancy degrees, it is something to be proud of as a beginner investor.

Look for index funds with low costs associated with them. I highly recommend starting off by looking into the ones offered by Vanguard.

If you believe that the American economy or whatever market index you are investing in will crash in the future, then do not invest in that market. But by investing in a market like the S&P 500, you are investing in the American economy which will likely not be going bankrupt anytime soon.

Remember that even if a market crash occurs then you have the opportunity to buy more at an even cheaper price. "Be fearful when others are greedy and greedy when others are fearful." – Warren Buffett

Before you start investing beyond index funds

There are simple steps you could take to prepare yourself for investing. Also, be sure to read over this book again before you start, especially the fundamentals and common mistakes sections:

Make a plan. Never go into investing without a proper investing plan. Not only will you perform worse, but it could also lead to significant losses. Because of that, take your time and really think about what you want to achieve. Examine different assets and learn about different sectors. See what you would like to invest in, and then create your long-term goals.

Always diversify but don't overdo it. A smart investor will recognize opportunities in different investing sectors. Just because you know a thing or two about technology, it doesn't necessarily mean you should put all your money there.

Diversification is key when it comes to building a balanced portfolio, so make sure you invest in a variety of stocks (which is likely what you will be starting off in) then move on to different asset classes as well. But, as mentioned before do not overdo it.

Always invest long-term. If you want to minimize fees and taxes in the case of stocks, then long-term investing is the best option. In terms of investing in general, it is far less stressful and it yields better returns. Maybe it is not as exciting as short-term buying and selling, but remember that the more boring investing is, the more likely it is working.

Do the proper research and believe in your judgment. If you have made the proper effort and researched all the details, then it is unlikely that your investments will perform poorly. Markets can be quite volatile but with the proper research, you don't have to panic every time prices drop.

Less is more. Most of the potential investment ideas you come across should be rejected. Remember that activity does not equal success in investing. In fact, the opposite is true. Look for an investment that really stands out and meets your criteria, and remember opportunity costs.

Invest with what you can afford. If you invest with only the money that you can afford losing, then you will always be in a more relaxed state which will lead to better investment decisions as well as a lot less headaches. Remember that emotions play a massive role in investing. By not making this mistake, you are already at an advantage for controlling your emotions.

Know yourself. I encourage you to try investing in different areas but if you realize that you are not emotionally ready for it (which is hard to admit!) then keep investing in index funds and just stick with it. Investing in powerful markets, such as the S&P 500 (and equivalents), will lead to amazing results over time through compounding.

The most important thing is to get started as soon as you can

In terms of investing, time is your most important asset due to how compounding works. Recall the different results from the example in chapter 2 that 5 years made in terms of the returns generated. Additionally, when you start early, you will have more time to save money. Not only does this mean that you will use compound interest to your advantage, but you will also be able to take more risks. Older people close to retirement often try to resist the temptation of investing heavily in equities and opt to invest in less risky investments such as bonds instead.

Taking on more risk does not mean you should not do the proper research and be sure of your investments. It means that even if you turn out to be wrong on an investment (after 2 years your investment still has not amounted to much), then you can afford that mistake. But, be sure to learn why it happened and how you can prevent it from happening again.

Make a checklist of all the mistakes that you make so you don't repeat them again. There is no need to fear losses if you train yourself to be an emotionless investor. In addition,

44

young adults can handle more pressure since retirement is generally still far away.

Investing isn't as complex as many perceive it to be. With proper knowledge and a will to learn, you too can create a lifestyle you have always wanted. Perseverance and time are the key points. By nurturing those traits, your wealth will grow every year.

Here are some more benefits to investing in your youth:

You will have a better lifestyle in the future. Most young adults have huge college debts they have to pay off. In addition, employment rates can be low, which can also influence their lifestyle. However, once you start investing the money you have, instead of spending it on things you don't need, you will soon start to see the results. Long-term investing means that you are investing in your future, and it will give you many opportunities you might not have even thought about. Even if you only invest with your standard paycheck, given enough time, you are looking at a lavish retirement plan, a new house, college funds for your children, and many other perks.[4][5][6]

You will curb your spending habits. Investing requires you to take a financial responsibility your parents might not have installed in you while you were a child. This often leads to

---

[4] http://www.ampcapital.com.au/resources/keys-to-successful-investing/why-it-pays-to-start-investing-early

[5] https://www.investopedia.com/financial-edge/0212/5-advantages-to-investing-in-your-20s.aspx

[6] https://www.veteransunited.com/money/5-reasons-to-start-investing-early/

irrational spending and barely making ends meet. Nevertheless, when you become an investor, you will follow a stricter budget and work towards your long term goals.

Start investing early on and create the lifestyle you have always wanted. Invest in yourself when you can, and never fear failure. I am certain that you will experience incredible results.

Conclusion

I hope you were able to get a well-founded introduction to investing and it's potential to propel you to new levels of wealth.

The next step is to keep expanding your knowledge by learning more and beginning to apply everything you learn. Application of knowledge is the difference between those that achieve success and those that simply watch.

If you have any questions, suggestions for me to add to the book, or suggestions for any other books you would like to see, then please do not hesitate to email me anytime at wwayne.publishing@gmail.com

Finally, if you enjoyed this book, then please feel free to leave a review. It would be very much appreciated!

Thank you and good luck on your journey to financial independence!

Bonus!

Please continue reading to learn more!

I am planning on writing more books that will dive deeper into investing into different asset classes, particularly stocks and real estate as these are the ones I have had the most success with. I will be sharing my strategies and all the lessons I have learned throughout the years in the same simple and straight forward manner as in this book. My goal is to help as many people as possible get a head start to achieve early retirement and financial independence so they can enjoy life without the worry of money.

From time to time, I write small articles, mini guides, tips and tricks, etc. that are not large enough to write a book on but important nonetheless. Additionally, I also let my subscribers know when I am releasing new material so they can be notified right away. As a thank you for subscribing, I have included a FREE gift. Here is the link: http://bit.ly/2GkBNz3

I look forward to sharing more value with you.

Cheers,

Walter

42359830R00028

Made in the USA
Lexington, KY
15 June 2019